Motorbikes

Experts on child reading levels
have consulted on the level of text and
concepts in this book.

At the end of the book is a "Look Back and Find" section
which provides additional information and encourages
the child to refer back to previous pages
for the answers to the questions posed.

Angela Grunsell trained as a teacher in 1969.
She has a Diploma in Reading and Related Skills
and for the last five years has advised London
teachers on materials and resources.
She worked for the ILEA as an advisory teacher
and currently works with teachers on
curriculum development in primary schools.

Published in the United States in 1986 by
Franklin Watts, 387 Park Avenue South, New York, NY10016

© Aladdin Books Ltd/Franklin Watts

Designed and produced by
Aladdin Books Ltd, 70 Old Compton Street, London W1

ISBN 0-531-10202-5

Printed in Italy
by Arti Grafiche Vincenzo Bona - Torino

FRANKLIN · WATTS · FIRST · LIBRARY

Motorbikes

by
Kate Petty

Consultant
Angela Grunsell

Illustrated by
Mike Saunders

Franklin Watts
New York · London · Toronto · Sydney

Do you think it would be exciting to ride
a little 50cc minibike like this
in a cross-country competition?

Or would you prefer to cruise down the highway
in comfort on a big Honda Goldwing 1200?
Two-wheeled transportation is fun,
but all riders wear crash helmets for safety.

Honda Goldwing 1200D

Even though they may look quite different on the outside, you will find the same basic parts on all motorbikes.

Kawasaki GPZ 600R

front suspension

disk brake

front brake lever

throttle

clutch

rear suspension spring

gas tank

exhaust pipe

engine

gear lever

Yamaha XT 350

chain

9

You use your whole body to control a heavy motorbike. You operate the rear brake and the gearshift with your feet, but most of the steering is done with your hands.

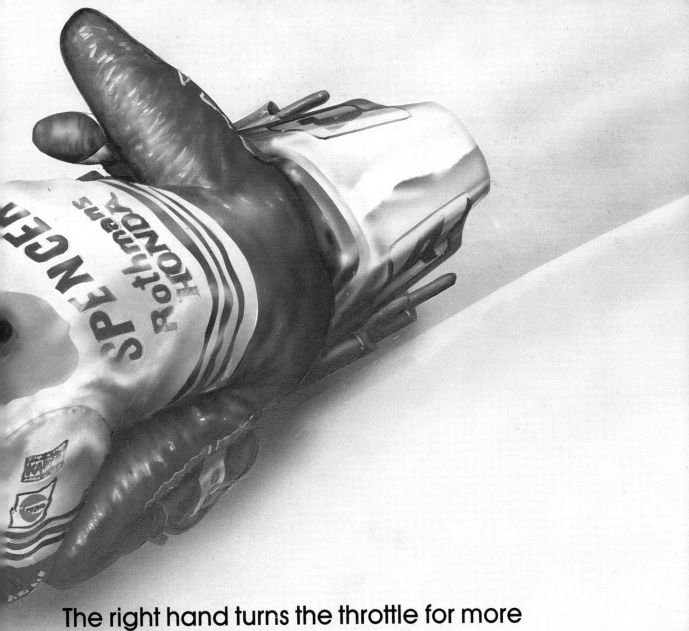

The right hand turns the throttle for more
speed and pulls the front brake lever to stop.
The left hand operates the clutch.

You see lightweight bikes like these everywhere.
They can dash through busy city traffic.
The engine and gas tank of a scooter
cannot be seen.

Puch Lido Vario

Beginners often start with a bike like the Yamaha 125. They can ride something more powerful, like the Gilera 250, when they have passed a driving test.

Gilera RV 250 NGR

Yamaha
DT 125 LC

All bikers have their favorite make of motorbike. Which do you like best? Kawasaki, Honda and Yamaha bikes are made in Japan.

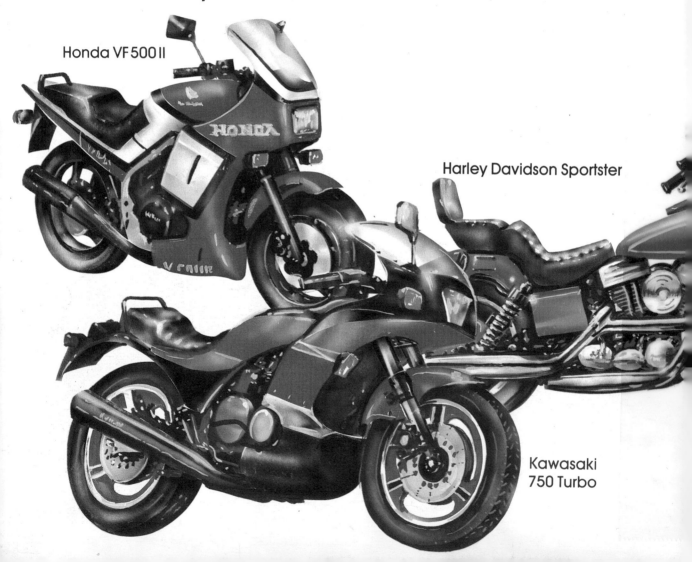

Honda VF 500 II

Harley Davidson Sportster

Kawasaki
750 Turbo

The Harley-Davidson company is famous for its enormous cruising bikes like the 1000cc Sportster. The German BMW even has an on-board computer which controls the engine.

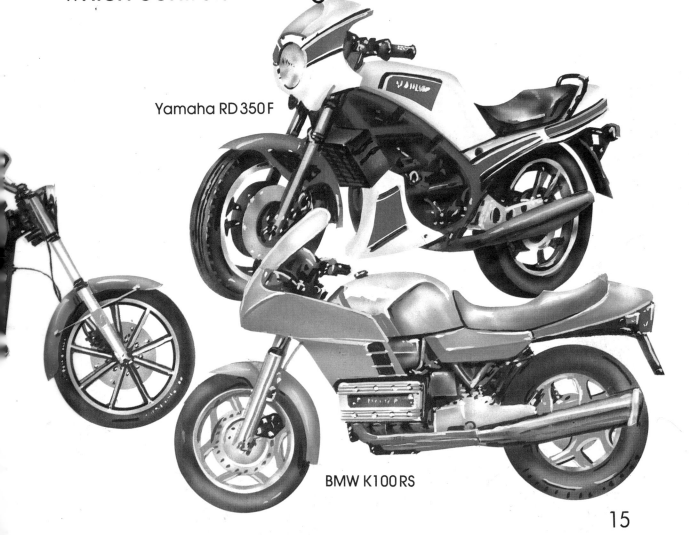

Yamaha RD 350 F

BMW K100 RS

Honda NS 400 R

Members of motorbike clubs organize races for
all classes of bikes. These are racing models
of road bikes – they can go on the racetrack
as well as on the road.

Bimota-Ducati DBI

Racing motorbikes need to be even more
streamlined than ordinary motorbikes.
The fairings on a racing bike cover almost
everything except the wheels and handlebars.

Grand Prix motorbike races are held all over the world. You can see how far the riders lean over without falling off. This is the best way to go around bends at fast speeds.

Grand Prix racing bikes are low and light.
They are fitted with smooth tires called slicks.
If it rains, slicks must be replaced immediately
by tires with tracks.

Yamaha 125 YX

Special bikes with knobby tires and good suspension are needed for this spectacular sport. Motocross competitors race, twist, turn and jump their bikes around a bumpy course.

Riders taking part in a Trials event might never go above 12 mph. They lose points if they stop or touch the ground, however rough the terrain. They need all their skill just to keep going.

Ice racing is a popular sport in countries where there is plenty of ice. The tires of ice-racing bikes are fitted with about 300 spikes.

Speedway racing is for professionals only – their bikes don't even have brakes! Four riders race around an oval cinder track. Sliding around bends like this is called "broadsliding."

Stunt riders are professionals who entertain spectators between races. Sometimes they leap through flames or jump over a row of buses. These two riders make a wheelie look effortless.

This dragster is jet-propelled! Dragsters are often built by their owners. They aim to race down a quarter-mile-long strip as fast as possible. This one can travel at more than 200 mph.

What skills do you need to compete in a Youth Motocross race like this, or in Youth Trials? You need a strong sense of balance and a good understanding of what you and your bike can do.

The riders all wear protective clothing
in case of an accident, but this sort
of racing is great fun.
Which rider do you think will win?

Look back and find

How do you make a motorbike go faster?

How do you stop?

What is a kick start?
You can stamp on a foot lever to start a motorbike once the ignition is on. Many bikes are now started electrically with a push button.

Where are lightweight bikes particularly useful?

How might you know that a 250cc Gilera is more powerful than the 125cc Yamaha?
The number of ccs (cubic centimeters) tells you about the size of the engine. An engine with a cubic capacity of 250ccs is more powerful than one with 125ccs.

What is special about the Kawasaki 750?
It has a turbo-charged engine which gives it extra power.

What does the computer do on the BMW?
It makes sure that exactly the right amount of fuel goes into the engine.

Why are the tires being changed?

How can you tell that this is a racing bike?

Why are slicks illegal on road bikes?
Slicks are dangerous on the road in wet weather and you can never be sure that it is not going to rain.

What sport is this?

Why does the bike need to have good suspension?
Good suspension makes a bumpy ride smoother and more comfortable.

How many riders take part in a speedway race?

What are they doing here?

What do speedway racers wear?
As well as the usual protective clothing they wear dust masks and a steel-capped left boot.

Index